Pickled Dreams Naked

Also by Norman Stock

Buying Breakfast For My Kamikaze Pilot
Salt Lake City: Gibbs Smith, Publisher, 1994.
(Winner of the 1993 Pregrine Smith Poetry Contest).

Pickled Dreams Naked

Norman Stock

The New York Quarterly Foundation, Inc.
New York, New York

NYQ Books™ is an imprint of The New York Quarterly Foundation, Inc.

The New York Quarterly Foundation, Inc.
P. O. Box 2015
Old Chelsea Station
New York, NY 10113

www.nyqbooks.org

Copyright © 2010 by Norman Stock

All rights reserved. No part of this book may be used or reproduced in any manner whatsoever without written permission of the author. This book is a work of fiction. Any references to historical events, real people or real locales are used fictitiously. Other names, characters, places, and incidents are products of the author's imagination, and any resemblance to actual events or locales or persons, living or dead, is entirely coincidental.

First Edition

Set in New Baskerville

Layout and Design by Raymond P. Hammond
Cover Art: "Pauper Dreams of True Love," 22" x 30", acrylic on paper
© 2007 Wen-hsien Wu, MD

Library of Congress Control Number: 2010907954

ISBN: 978-1-935520-30-6

for Lydia

Acknowledgments

These poems first appeared in the following publications:

"Give Us This Day," *Barrow Street*.

"Trying to Remember Himself at 18," *College English*.

"Again," "I Only Remember the Good Parts," "Standing Room Only," *Hanging Loose*.

"A Yarmulke," *Home Planet News*.

"The Application," *The New Republic*.

"At the Bottom of the Mountain," "From the Grass to the Sea," "Homage to Ogden Nash," "The Last Straw," "The Lesson of the Poetry Workshop," "My Poetry Reading," "The night about me restless," "The Poem Eaten as Written," "Prosaic," "ship his body back," "There's Hope for Us Yet," "Time Marches On," "Wallace Stevens in Queens," "Wallace Stevens Smokes a Cigar," *The New York Quarterly*.

"What I Said," *Poetry After 9/11: An Anthology of New York Poets*. (Hoboken: Melville House, 2002).

"In the Chicken Shop," "Subway Heaven," *Skidrow/Penthouse*.

"Chicken History," "Dog Day," *The Styles*.

"Kafka's Lawsuit," "Striking a Balance," *Verse*.

"Can I Untangle Your Hair," "Modus Operandi de W. S.," *Whereas*.

These poems also appeared in the following publications:

"The Application," reprinted in *Anthology of Magazine Verse and Yearbook of American Poetry*, 1997 edition. (Palm Springs: Monitor Book Company, 1997).

"The Lesson of the Poetry Workshop," reprinted in *New Plains Review* (Fall, 2008).

"What I Said," reprinted in *Poetry: An Introduction*, by Michael Meyer. Fourth edition. (Boston: Bedford/St. Martin's, 2004). Also reprinted in *The Bedford Introduction to Literature*, by Michael Meyer. Seventh edition. (Boston: Bedford/St. Martin's, 2005) and *The Compact Bedford Introduction to Literature*, by Michael Meyer. Eighth edition. (Boston: Bedford/St. Martin's, 2008).

Some of the poems in this book were written in William Packard's legendary poetry workshop in the late '60s and early '70s, the period when he founded *The New York Quarterly*. Thanks to his abiding influence and to his outstanding successor as editor of *NYQ*, Raymond Hammond, for his masterly work in editing, producing, and publishing this book.

My gratitude also to my former teachers: David Ignatow, William Matthews, and James Tate, and special thanks for invaluable help with the manuscript at various stages to Molly Peacock, Geoffrey Nutter, and Charles Harper Webb.

Contents

I

Kafka's Lawsuit   / 15
The Application   / 16
Prosaic   / 17
Give Us This Day   / 18
What I Said   / 19
At Ground Zero   / 20
New York: Save for Later   / 21
I Only Remember the Good Parts   / 22
The Exploding Suitcase   / 23
Myself on Halloween   / 24
Incident on West 24th Street   / 25
Plucked   / 26
Onward with Cookie   / 27
Trying to Remember Himself at 18   / 28
In the Mall   / 29
I Know, I Know   / 30
Dog Day   / 31
Hound of Earth   / 32
In the Chicken Shop   / 33
Eating Chicken from the Grave   / 34
Chicken History   / 35
The Bad Teacher Wins   / 37
The Lesson of the Poetry Workshop   / 38
The Madness of Art   / 39
No Ideas but in Things   / 40
At a Boring Poetry Reading   / 41
The Words Anyone Has to Say   / 42

II

Time Marches On / 45
Go / 46
Plaint / 47
all he has / 48
Put Up or Shut Up / 49
The Beggars / 50
Money Song / 52
As a Fat Man Turning / 53
Standing Room Only / 54
We Appreciate Your Patience / 55
The Tall Woman of Dreams / 56
the night about me restless / 57
Can I Untangle Your Hair / 58
Wrong Way Joe / 59
The Way Things Happen / 60
Again / 61
Unyielding / 62
And/Or / 63
To Be Sung at Dusk / 64
Take It / 65
From the grass to the sea / 66
Poetry Bread / 67
Homage to Ogden Nash / 68
Modus Operandi de W. S. / 69
Wallace Stevens Smokes a Cigar / 70
The Poem Eaten as Written / 71
My Poetry Reading / 72
The Famous Chicken / 73

III

A Yarmulke / 77
There's Hope for Us Yet / 78
Striking a Balance / 79
I Said to the Wind / 80
This / 81
ship his body back / 82
The Last Thing / 84
Quandary / 85
If He Wants Us, He Can Have Us / 86
Options / 87
To My Transplanted Kidney / 88
Subway Heaven / 89
The Oldest Philosopher in the World / 90
The Summoning / 92
When it Matters / 93
With the Thousand-Year-Old Woman / 94
Amazing Queens / 95
Wallace Stevens in Queens / 96
How to Become the Poet Laureate of Queens / 97
What They Want / 99
At the Bottom of the Mountain / 100
The Last Straw / 101
Rant / 102
Reflections on Names in the News / 103
Draconian Measures / 104

Pickled Dreams Naked

I

Kafka's Lawsuit

Kafka returns from the grave and sues all writers who sound like him for plagiarism. Being familiar with the intricacies of the law and a man gifted with words, his case, on paper, seems quite strong. The judge, however, is not impressed. "After all," the judge says, "sounding like you may not be plagiarism at all. It may be necessary due to the condition of our lives."

"But your honor," says Kafka, removing his hat out of deference to the judge, "my technique of writing has become the favorite tool of mere charlatans who know nothing of the nature of the world."

The judge looks at Kafka severely. "And do you assert," he says, "that you alone know the nature of the world and what it sounds like to write about it?"

"Only that many are imitating my technique, such as it is, your honor," Kafka replies. " I only request the damages due to me for this injustice, this copy-catism that is using my work in a wrongheaded and quite inappropriate manner."

"You are an arrogant man," the judge says, "and I rule against you without even considering your specious argument. One look at you standing there with your hat in your hand and I knew that you would not win your case. You are not fit for a court of law, and even less fit for the world."

"But your honor," says Kafka, "my fitness is not the question."

"And since when do you decide what the question is?" demands the judge. "Do you not realize that this has been your problem all along? Take this man away!" he orders the bailiff. "Case dismissed!" And the judge sits back happy, satisfied that he has once again made the right decision in the case of Kafka.

The Application

coming at last to the
bureaucracy of being
office of what is
I bring the paper
to the chief of operations
who says it is not
correctly prepared
and sends me to the tenth room
on the fortieth floor
where I am to ask for
a mister noosebaum
who will give me permission
to resubmit my application
if I so desire
and if not I can go
to the twelfth room
on the twenty-seventh floor
and sign a document
that will absolve me of responsibility
for my original application
which was incorrectly prepared
and is now invalid
with no hope of being accepted
nothing else will be granted
unless I proceed
according to instructions

Prosaic

the smelly feet of poetry
the running nose the ripped trousers
the bleeding pimples the disfigured faces
of the sick is what poetry
is trying to get at, the sonnet about nothing at all that is beautiful
disorganized elbows and old people asleep
the covers covering them the comforts of infants
is what poetry must make itself out of, there isn't anything else

Give Us This Day

>*"For every star on Broadway,*
>*there's a salami sandwich."*
>
>Red Buttons, on "Larry King Live"

stuck between each every day
I am the cold cut hanging
in the delicatessen of the starving
the handmade meat and daily bread
of the unsatisfied give us then
for every broken heart on Broadway
something good to eat that is me and my
beaten body me and my pickled dreams naked
on your mustard skin me and my hopes
barely held together in your hungry hand

What I Said

after the terror I
went home and cried and
said how could this happen and
how could such a thing be and
why why I mean how could
anything so horrible and how could
anyone do such a thing to us and what
will happen next and how can we live now
it's impossible to understand it's impossible
to do anything after this and what will any of us do now and how will we
    live and how can we expect to go on after this
I said and I said this is too much to take no one can take a thing like this
after the terror yes and then I said let's kill them

At Ground Zero

what remains
remains
what is
is
what vanishes
vanishes
and you
you are still who you are

New York: Save for Later

give it a groundbreaking
give it a big cigar
give it my heart in my hand the holes in my shoes
New York, save for later, throw it all away
give it my uncle's long winded worshipping of the bitch goddess success
give it that, give it up, give it all away
you know her, New York, give her the crime of the century
my aching balls, the rabbit's foot, the fast moving metaphor
take it, take it, take it away from me
New York of the rabble, throw them in the trough eat them
you wanted them, you got them, here they all are gaping
take 72nd street, take 5th avenue, take Brooklyn
let 'em eat cake, this is New York, go break bread with the innocent
what do you care, what do you want, what do you think you will get
a fist in the face that's what, a good hard right to the stomach
fall on the floor New York, get up and be beaten again
you expected everything and you sure did get it all
New York of the towers, of the homegrown idiots, of the torn flowers

I Only Remember the Good Parts

me and benny went and took
arlene's glasses off her face
then we ran around the corner to an empty lot
near benny's house where we smashed
the glasses by jumping up and down on them
till they were nothing but little pieces
then we went upstairs to benny's house
to watch television in the living room
which is what we were doing when arlene's mother
came in with her two shaggy white dogs
she was a funny looking woman with a round face and glasses
and she smelled of her dogs and all I can remember
is her standing there with the dogs and looking at us

The Exploding Suitcase

my mother carries a suitcase
in it is my life
the suitcase opens and I come out screaming
so my mother puts me back in and slams the suitcase shut

now I got a real problem now that I'm alive
how to get out of the suitcase and yet keep her carrying me
this is the mystery of the ages and it is between me and everyone else
this back and forth this leaping out and being shut back in

carry me then to the grave mother carry me to the sky
let me lie on a cloud with a harp in my hand just so you keep me in the
    suitcase just so you keep it with you forever

Myself on Halloween

I write you a picture of myself on Halloween
how I come disguised as somebody else's son
going from door to door with my child's hand exposed
but inside I am myself who knows the ropes and more
okay so you give me candy I take it and I eat
no child except I disguise myself as the child I was to be
no matter what you give me I know who I am
my trick is to treat you as you are and I am not

Incident on West 24th Street

I sat in the hallway crying
because Heshy hit me
or it looked like Heshy hit me

but he didn't really hit me
what he did was tell me he didn't want
to be my friend anymore that's what made me cry

so when my father hit Heshy for hitting me
he wasn't entirely wrong in doing that
although he was entirely wrong in doing that

and when Heshy's mother gave my father a court summons for it
she was right to do so but not entirely right
and it was good that Jenny Markowitz talked her out of it

because if she hadn't they might have hauled us all into court
me my father Heshy his mother our nosy neighbor Mrs. Gemberg
and God knows who else to try and find out who hit who and why when all I wanted

was for Heshy who hadn't hit me to begin with to keep on being my friend
which is what did happen anyway and one week later my aunt Miriam pointed to the
    two of us
Heshy and me sitting in an abandoned car and laughing and she said look who's so
    friendly now

Plucked

o I was a boy once
that fleeting smile
looked at myself naked in a mirror
touched my body my cock and balls
and I said I am a boy
for I was indeed a weed of a boy
now I am a man
no more *mirrors* please

Onward with Cookie

I had a heated argument
with my friend Cookie when I was
eleven years old about which part of a girl
was the best part he said the tits I said the ass
we rattled on and on about this and about our fantasies
and what we would like to do to girls and finally Cookie said the ass is good
and I said yeah I like tits and we kind of shook
hands on it good friends to the last as onward we went

Trying to Remember Himself at 18

cunt starved
tit hungry
ass backwards

dying every day
out of his fucking mind
and yet somehow happy

jerking off in the morning
jerking off in the evening
jerking off in the afternoon

hand-to-mouth philosopher
he needs a job
will somebody give this fucking kid a fucking job

shit faced snot nosed
idiot adolescent forever
o please enough already

In the Mall

so there was this girl
with a tight tee shirt
coming toward me
incredibly big tits
for such a small girl
sticking right out
and on the shirt it said
right over her tits
hello boys
in big black letters
I had to smile
what was she selling
or was she just being friendly

I Know, I Know

going blind on the bus
after hitting my fucking head
or so I thought, what's life
going blind? seeing clear?
what's death? shutting down?
who knows, I'm here
that's all I ever see
blind me, blind me
why can't I open up
and look at what's really here
a whole world, yeah yeah
tell me about it

Dog Day

A dog is crying outside my window. I throw a cardboard box at it; won't it ever shut up. The dog responds to the box by barking at the window. Son of a bitch! I'll teach him.

I go down with a stick to beat the dog. When I get to the street, the dog is not there. Instead, I am confronted by a gang of teenage hoodlums. "What you wan', jojo?" they ask with threatening looks.

"Uh...there was this dog down here making noise," I say, "I couldn't sleep."

"Oh yeah, hot shot. You lookin' to sleep?" and one of them comes real close, grinning and jabbing at me.

Suddenly I am hit in the back with the cardboard box. I turn around, and there is the dog, at the end of a chain held by one of the hoods. The dog looks at me as though he knows me. He makes a move toward me, but is violently pulled back by the young punk holding him.

"So you wanna sleep, eh Charlie?" says the grinning hood again.

"Not really," I say, "I mean, not here. If you'll excuse me, I'll be going now." And I turn to leave, but they close in around me in a ring.

"I'll take that stick now, buddy boy," says the hood.

"Why sure, I didn't mean anything," I say, trying to wheedle my way out. Then the thug takes the chain off the dog and slips it around my waist. "What's this?" I ask.

"Momo, you're joining our club now. You're gonna be one of us. Don't that soun' good?" says the hood, who is now holding the stick I came down with. As he raises the stick to beat me, I bark loudly at him, as loud as I can. Then the dog, which is now unchained, leaps at the hood in a fury, biting the hand holding the stick. The rest of the gang attacks, but they are sent scattering in all directions by the wildly snapping, manic dog, which has become a ferocious beast. When they are gone, I am still barking, but as the dog gently approaches me, I begin to whimper and finally to cry, just as he was crying before. We embrace like old friends.

Hound of Earth

dog of no virtues
why do you follow me
through the unending city
you run with your dog breath
pissing on the walls of the mighty
you are a naughty dog
carousing with the bitches of the evening
dog self that I didn't want
how did you attach yourself to me
that I follow you dog-like
even as you follow me
through every alley and garbage heap
you are my man my dog
my one and only wish for myself
that I be worthy of your doggedness
through the pitfalls of history
the hell-holes and wicked streets
where we assemble our tawdry human selves
you and I my dog
all these drastic dog-worn days
you and I enter the rapaciousness of the present moment
and if the big dog catcher in the sky comes to get you
I will try to protect you my animal
I will keep you from the human arsenal

In the Chicken Shop

I sit in the chicken
shop and I think of
how I am empty
how I am nothing
soon I will eat and
feed my own nothing
not be so empty
here in the chicken
shop where I look for
somewhere a waiter
to bring me water
to bring me chicken
here in the empty
shop where I chicken
out my existence
waiting for water

Eating Chicken from the Grave

everything tastes like chicken, even death
if it has a taste, chewy and bland and chicken-like
cluck cluck cluck go the death birds of the innocent earth
they say lay you down and they say we will shit on your head
we are the chicken bones of your life and we are no longer yours
you ate us and you ate us and you will continue to eat us
from the chicken grave of your life your head pokes up into our entrails
taste us now, this nothingness, like the death that you didn't want, and eat
    eat eat, eat to your heart's content

Chicken History

A chicken walked into a factory and asked for a job. The factory manager said, "Get out of here, you are a chicken."

"But I need a job," said the chicken.

"I don't employ chickens in this factory," said the manager.

Then a bolt of lightning came out of the blue and struck down the manager. He lay at the chicken's feet, and there were no witnesses to what had occurred. At this point, one of the factory workers came in and saw the manager on the floor in front of the chicken. "What happened?" he asked.

"The manager has been struck by lightning and killed," said the chicken, "but before he died, he appointed me to replace him. I am now the manager of this factory."

Seeing the manager lying there and the chicken announcing his appointment with such confidence, the worker went to spread the news to the other workers. Since the previous manager had been tyrannical and mean-spirited, the workers were at first happy to get a new manager. The chicken, however, while possessing some excellent management skills, turned out to be just as bad. Nevertheless, the factory grew and prospered. It was known as the Factory of the Chicken.

One day, a familiar looking man walked into the chicken's office. After a brief discussion, the man pulled a hatchet out of his back pocket and chopped off the chicken's head. He took the head out to the factory and made a formal proclamation to the workers. "I am the manager," he said, "the one you thought struck dead by lightning. Actually, I was not killed, only immobilized for several years. Now I am back, and I have killed this lying chicken."

"But the chicken said you had appointed him manager," said the workers.

"That was a lie," said the manager, "and the chicken has paid for it with his life."

Suddenly the chicken's headless body, which had been hopping about wildly, came into the factory and bumped the manager in the ass, knocking him into a vat of gooey chocolate where he drowned.

The workers then decided to run the factory without a manager. The chicken's head was combined with the chocolate covered body of the manager to serve as the newly run factory's logo. It became known as the Factory of the Chicken Head and Chocolate Body. This factory is now famous all over the world for the beauty of its products, the happiness of its workers, and the distinctiveness of its pictorial trademark, whose origin is now long buried in the annals of chicken history.

The Bad Teacher Wins

the teacher will want
to make an example of me
he will flog me naked in front of the class
and make me recite my lessons by heart
bad teacher I hate you
die if you touch me death to you
yet here I stand naked and flogged
saying my lessons for all the world

The Lesson of the Poetry Workshop

I have a problem with this poem
and my problem is you you miserable person
sitting here in this godforsaken poetry workshop trying to become
    famous
don't you know that only the teacher is famous and that that's what
    poetry workshops are all about
they are about the teacher not you you awful wreck of a person trying
    to get published
don't you know that only the teacher gets published come off it
get out of here already nobody wants your horrible poems
all anybody ever wants is the teacher's poems and you keep coming back
    when will you ever learn

The Madness of Art

I decided to write terrible poems
first it was just an idea, then it became an obsession
they came pouring out of me, one after another
so many, I didn't know I had such incompetence in me
horrible stuff, hackneyed images, repetitious rants
the worst rhetoric you could conceive of, and yet I kept on writing them
no one could stop me, they said, what are you doing
you are making a fool of yourself, you are writing poems that are not
    worthy of your talent
what talent, I said, this is the real me
this terrible poet, this inexpressibly horrible mess of a man
this is me, there is no other, there is no way back
then they put me in a cage, and they said, no more poetry from you
you are a threat to the civilized world, you sully all that is beautiful with
    your awful poems
all right, I said, all right, if you let me out I will stop writing poems
so they let me out, and I ran away, where no one could find me
and I kept on writing my gibberish, my uncomplicated messages, my
    wonderful horrible rhymes and riddles because there was no
    way for me to stop

No Ideas but in Things

don't be abstract
stick to fact
say what's known
be concrete
like a stone
in the street
like a brick
that you kick
like a leaf
that you tear
like the life
that you wear
like the thing
that you are

At a Boring Poetry Reading

They read the audience to death.
These poets use live ammunition, their words, to weaken us.
Are they trying to put us to sleep or are they trying to keep themselves up
by droning on and on? Instead of listening, all I'm doing is waiting for them to stop.
The applause will be like glass breaking, the glass they are enclosing us in.
It is as if they tied their shoes in front of us just to show us they could tie their shoes
    in front of us!
O save me from this scatterbrain orderliness, this posture of beheading.
Will this reading never end? Will I have to listen forever
or can I find a chink in the wall of my own mind that I can crawl into, just to get
    away from this disaster, this dying, this voicelessness?

The Words Anyone Has to Say

so much depends
on the words anyone has to say
and how they say them
and if they are appropriate
to the situation they are saying them about
and if the situation requires words to be said about it
because if they are the wrong words
and if they are not said in the right way
and if they do not fit the situation or are required to be said by it
then whoever said them should have kept their damn mouths shut

II

II

Time Marches On

I have a feeling about you
but I don't really want to say it
for one thing, you might not appreciate what I say
and for another, what I say about you may be totally wrong
but I guess I'll have to say it anyway
so here it is: you're an idiot
I have felt this way about you for a long time
and now that you know, I hope you won't hold it against me,
    idiot that you are

Go

go get a better life
where don't ask me
what are you stupid or
what are you fucking dumb
go get another way
whatsamatter jackass
can't you figure it out
kick in the head is what you need
go get a finer thing
than this old harrowing
what are you incapable
kick in the head is what you need

Plaint

what I don't understand
is how much I have to do to do
any part of it it all seems so difficult
and difficulty is not something I want

I want everything to be simple to be understood
simply I want to be able to accept
what I must accept without it being difficult
why is it that it seems so difficult

for me to do any of it why is that the way it is
why does it all seem so hard especially for me to do

when I think about it everything becomes so complicated
how can I do any of it it seems impossible I give up

all he has

all he has
he puts in bags
that he gives to boys
who give the bags to other boys
then the girls come
they take the bags and throw them in the air
all he has goes sailing up to the clouds
he loves it like that
it is how he lives

Put Up or Shut Up

put your money
where your mouth is
put your mouth
where it will do the most good
put your good
where your money is not
put your mouth
where it must never go
put where you must never go
where your money is mouthing itself
higher and higher
till you break the bank
the bank where your money grows
and the river where your mouth flows
over its banks
over its many many riverbanks
and where you
your little self
gets stronger and stronger
as only money can make you
and let your mouth run
with the flow of your money
till there is no more left
neither money nor mouth
and you will be forgotten
you and your money
you and your mouth
you and all you ever were
money and mouth
mouth and money
nothing ever again
not a trace of you left

The Beggars

I am told her house is at the end of an alley, The alley is full of tin cans, stray cats, and homeless beggars sleeping against the walls. I walk by on tiptoe, trying not to wake the beggars. But as I step quietly along, I accidentally kick a tin can, which makes a clattering sound. The sound seems to annoy some of the cats, who begin yowling. All this noise, naturally, wakes up the beggars, the one thing I was trying to avoid.

"Spare any change?" a fat beggar in a rather picturesque outfit asks.

"No," I say, hurrying along.

"What do you mean no," says another beggar, this one sporting a sleek white beard.

I walk faster, trying to ignore them. The alley seems endless. Where is that stupid house of hers, I keep thinking. Just as one of the beggars charges across the alley and lunges at me, I step out into the light.

I am in a street that is flooded with light, but her house is nowhere to be seen. Then she appears next to me, as if she were there all along. "Were you here all along?" I ask.

She does not answer, but leads me to her house, which is in another street. When we enter, I see the beggars I left in the alley seated at a large table having dinner.

"What are they doing here?" I ask, stepping back, getting ready to run out.

"These are my guests," she says, "just as you are my guest. Did you think I only invited you?"

The beggar with the white beard turns, pulls up a chair, and tells me gruffly to sit down. "You would not give us anything in the alley, but now, in this good woman's house, we will welcome you as a fellow guest," he says, staring at me with a full-faced intensity that makes me lower my head in shame.

The other beggar, the fat one in the picturesque outfit, turns on me. "Are you uncomfortable sitting at a table with beggars? Think a minute, perhaps you are a beggar yourself," he says.

"Now, now, " she says finally, "let's not have any arguments in my house. I have asked you all here for a pleasant visit, not to fight."

I get up from my chair, feeling naked and exposed, a shamefaced beggar among beggars. "If you will excuse me," I say, my head lowered, "I do not feel well and must leave now." And I bolt for the door, almost knocking her over in my rush to get out. But the door will not open, and I am stuck where I stand, my hand grasping the knob, and all eyes fixed on me.

"No," says the white-bearded beggar, "you will stay. And you will eat with beggars for once, and you will learn to be a man."

Shamefaced, I return to the table, lift my fork with the rest of them, and begin to eat.

Money Song

money money everywhere
in the sky and in the sea
everywhere, it's just money
falling from the leaves and trees
all the different currencies
down they come and up they go
it's a constant undertow
everywhere I look I see
every kind of currency
it's too much to get and spend
will it ever have an end
only in the grave where you
will have spent all that you're due

As a Fat Man Turning

as a fat man turning
seeing his shadow seeing how fat he is
with that gesture of contempt
saying I know I am fat but still I am
and having turned even now my large body
he turns and he gives that look of pride mixed with regret

Standing Room Only

holy bless
the subway mob
I push into
like a kid who doesn't
know up from down
the subway lurch
of the mob and me
we love each other
like child and mother
who ride it out
forever and ever

We Appreciate Your Patience

if this subway
were not a subway
if this subway were an open field
I would run and breathe in that open field
instead of being stuck in this stalled train with heat to breathe
    instead of air to breathe
if the world would end now
then it would deserve to end now
the way this subway
continues to be a subway
and does not change into an open field
and does not allow me to run and breathe in an open field

The Tall Woman of Dreams

there was a woman who was so tall she was invisible
you walked through her legs in the daylight
you trampled her breasts at night
she was not there and yet she encompassed everything
one day you hit her knee so hard with the top of your head that you
    wondered
have I broken off a piece of the sky or have I invented a new ceiling
but then you realized it was only part of the large body of the daylight
her body, the woman whose size was infinite and who was all over
    everything and everywhere

the night about me restless

the night about me restless
the day like a loose shawl falling

from the shoulders of some impossible woman
I being who I am arranging

the distance and the slowness and covering
her up, so she will not be seen or noticed or known

Can I Untangle Your Hair

can I untangle your hair that is so beautiful or must I wait
can I if I want to do as I want to

your hair that is so beautiful
can I untangle your hair that is so beautiful

or must I wait till you say yes I can
or must I wait or can I now do as I want to

and untangle your hair that is so beautiful
or must I wait till you say yes I can

Wrong Way Joe

I said I'd wait
and wait I did
she said track 10
this was track 10
but where was she
no way to know
a bad mistake
is what it was
and yet I stood
for four hard hours
without a thought
of what to do
and all the time
she had it right
and went to where
she meant to go
but not with me
a sorry sight
still waiting for
god damn it, her!

The Way Things Happen

sometimes your life is like a wave
the way it happens and it's not
something you can control or stop

you love a woman who you leave
and then it's she comes back to you
years later, and it just goes on

the way it was, and this is what
you think of when you think of it
the time it takes for things to be

and change, the way a wave can break
against a rock and then go on
as water, which it always was

Again

she came back I said ok let's
do it so we did we did it
that was good I said hey let's do
it again she said ok let's
do it again if you like so
we did it again it was good
it's really nice to be with you
again I said and she said yes
it was and it was so we did
it again that's what's good about
life sometimes you can do it and
then do it again I mean just
because it was once over once
doesn't mean it's over for good
she came back and it was ok

Unyielding

when the horses take you
you will be a horse
when the camels take you
you will be a camel
when the fire engine takes you
you will be a fire engine
but when I take you
you will be yourself
and when you take me
I will be myself
and we will both fly away like that
unyielding, not knowing the consequence

And/Or

for what was said
and what was not
you heard and did
or you did not

for what was meant
and what was not
you understood
or you did not

and now that time
has given up
for what was said
and what was not

you know at last
and you do not
all that was meant
or you do not

To Be Sung at Dusk

that the reddest flower
be pulled from its place
and torn into pieces
and me eat the pieces
that you give me, that you give me
because you love to see me eat them
with such ardor as the bird in the bug house
the horse in the high hay, the fish in the wide water

Take It

there's a way
that for you
is the way

there's a time
that for you
is the time

there's a place
that for you
is the place

but you must
hurry there
hurry there

From the grass to the sea

From the grass to the sea
Takes an hour and a half by foot if you walk

And one man by land if you run and one intricate hour
In the long lost moon's light in the sun's heat

If you stagger, and one tremendous cycle
Of winds and seasons, if you forget to go.

Poetry Bread

it's what you knead
from the flour
of your words
it leavens out
and rises as
your only hope
that you will chew
like you did once
your blanket in
the dark of night
afraid to sleep
afraid not to

Homage to Ogden Nash

What could be dumber
Than rhyming? I mean, even someone from Philadelphia who dresses up in a funny costume and black face and calls himself a mummer
Would have to admit that putting words together so they rhyme is really so dumb that there's just about nothing you could think of that could be thought of as dumber

Ask any mummer

I mean, I wouldn't do a stupid rhymed poem for love or money or even may god help me cold honest cash
And I'm sure that what's-his-name who this poem is actually about wouldn't either because he wouldn't want to be caught doing something that could be considered trash

Not Ogden Nash

And though some people say that he rhymed with great art
I would prefer to think that what he actually did was ridicule the whole thing by making his rhymes so outlandish as if he was saying look how dumb it is to rhyme and while some people would still say that's rhyming I don't I say it's handling a bad poetic tradition in a way that I consider to be astonishingly smart

Modus Operandi de W. S.

Wallace Stevens
Always evens

Out the edges
Wallace hedges

Über alles
Always Wallace

Stevens evens
Out his grievance.

Wallace Stevens Smokes a Cigar

The aroma of this cigar
Beats all philosophy

To smithereens, and shatters
The hammers of my hearing

I believe in
Smoking cigars

To lighten the heavy burden
Of imagined angels falling.

The Poem Eaten As Written

thrust your tongue into it
the cunt world of poetry
the bittersweet mother meat
bite into it bite into it good
then spit out your broken teeth
and be glad your tongue has not yet been torn out
fool, you thought you were only writing a poem
and now your mouth is full of blood and you will spit shit forever

My Poetry Reading

my poetry reading is all of a piece with my life and there is no escape
my poetry reading is written in the sky in white letters and disappears in puffs of smoke
my poetry reading makes the cigars fall out of the mouths of tired businessmen
my poetry reading scares the pants off the professors and sends them climbing the walls asking forgiveness
my poetry reading is a girl in a very short skirt whose legs extend forever
my poetry reading needs help will someone please call the fire department
my poetry reading is becoming ill with a pain in the right foot is there a doctor in the house
my poetry reading bears a child in February and gives out cigars to the audience
my poetry reading was conceived in absentia by a man on death row and no pardon is possible
my poetry reading is in the back of your mind, sister, do not deny it
my poetry reading is a pig with an apple in its mouth but why are we celebrating now
my poetry reading is owned by a woman in the back row who glares at me in silence
my poetry reading needs no excuse but I am sorry anyway
my poetry reading cries all night and I hold it in my arms and I comfort it

The Famous Chicken

Everybody wanted to see the famous chicken. People were lining up even before the sun rose to be sure they got a good view. The arena was decked out with flags and banners, special security forces were in evidence in strategic locations, and there was a feeling of tremendous excitement that was almost palpable in the very air. This was, after all, one of the few times that the general public would be in proximity, to see, if they were lucky, maybe even to touch, the famous chicken. But it was just this last eventuality that was putting the whole enterprise in jeopardy. "No hands," the chicken insisted to his managers, "absolutely no hands. If they can't stand at a respectful distance and look, then I will not appear. I mean, I don't mind being looked at, in fact, I rather like it. But I will not, I repeat not, allow my body to be touched. Not so much as one feather!"

"Fucking bird," one of the managers was heard muttering in a hallway at the side of the arena. "We set him up, we make him into something big, and right away he begins to put on airs."

"Yeah," said another one of the managers—there were hundreds of managers—"why can't he just be a chicken, why does he have to act holier-than-thou?"

When the gates opened, the people poured in like an unruly mob, but as they entered the arena and got closer to the center of attraction, a strange stillness came over each one of them. They were, after all, in the presence of the famous chicken! There was a large curtain around the center of the arena, and the people sat in silence waiting for it to be opened. Then, with a fanfare and roll of drums, the curtain began going up. There were gasps and sighs from all around as the chicken's head came into view, followed by the right wing, the left wing, and then, at last, the tail. The chicken was encircled by a wire mesh fence intended to protect him from the crowd. Fascinated by the sight of him, the people edged closer and closer to the fence. There was a flurry among the managers, a rush to try to protect, and then a stepping back to see what was actually happening.

Before there was time to do anything about it, however, the crowd had burst forth from its previous mood of restrained silence and was all over the wire fence. Not only did they stick their fingers in to try to touch the chicken, but many were climbing on the top part to peer down at it. While they couldn't touch it, they were close enough for the chicken to feel their hot breath and to see their drooling mouths. Needless to say, the chicken was aghast at this spectacle. He remembered the old days, when people had some respect for famous chickens and kept their hands and their eyes and their mouths to themselves. It was at times like these that he would recall his youth, when his parents would say of him, "he will be a famous chicken." And now, look what it had all come to. Ah, fame, what ambiguities you inspire, he thought.

Then it happened. The fence collapsed from the weight of the people and they fell in on top of the chicken. They grabbed and tore at his body, and before long the chicken's head was mashed to shreds, his feathers were torn to pieces, his little legs were pulled out and crushed to nothing. The whole personality of the chicken virtually disappeared as his body was dismantled bone by bone at the hands of the frantic, half-crazed multitude. After a brief attempt to intervene, the managers saw that it was no use. "We have lost our chicken," they said mournfully.

III

A Yarmulke

I am alive for a reason
but I don't know the reason
so I went to the rabbi
and I said, what is the reason
the rabbi spit in my face
he said, you have to ask
gee, I said, a Zen master rabbi
for this I would even wear a yarmulke

There's Hope for Us Yet

I saw this young Muslim woman
outside the Queens Library in Jamaica
wearing a hijab, the traditional headscarf
but also in tight red pants and high heels
with real sexy skinny legs and laughing
things are looking up, I thought
maybe the clash of civilizations is not what it appears to be
maybe the end of the world is not really at hand
I'll take her, minus the hijab, or better yet keep it on
just wrap those skinny Muslim legs around my hungry Jewboy body
    and everything will be all right

Striking a Balance

A door opens and a demon walks into the room. I speak to the demon as if he is my friend, but he refuses to answer. When I say hello the demon looks away and when I ask him how he is he does not answer. It is typically demonic of him to be this way, I think, and I will not hold him accountable. Still, I have to deal with the demon somehow. Thinking about this for a while, I finally hit on a strategy: I will let the demon come to me.

Sitting back in my comfortable chair, I begin to ignore the demon. I read a book or file my nails or busy myself with some papers on my desk. The demon watches all this somewhat nervously, and begins inching toward me. As he gets closer, I read my book with more concentration, or busy myself harder with my paperwork. Soon the demon has come so close he almost touches me. At this point I look up, stare straight into his face, and say, in triumph, "aha!"

The demon blushes a dark red at my having caught him at his own game. He lowers his head and looks sheepishly up at me from the corner of his demonic eye. "Did you not think I was on to you," I say to him triumphantly.

The demon opens his mouth as if to speak but then thinks better of it. He steps away gingerly, turns his back to me and slowly, ever so slowly, with small demonic steps, leaves the room.

Well, I think, settling back in my comfortable chair, he'll be back. Not that I need him or want him, but one can't be too careful either playing into the hands of demons or staying entirely free of them. A balance must be struck, and it's always good to be one up on demons. Which I felt I was now, and I sat back with a feeling of real satisfaction, although I could still hear his footsteps outside my door, like an uncertain mouse not sure if he should enter or if he should leave altogether.

I Said to the Wind

I said to the wind
be my friend
and the wind said
no go

I said to the sun
warm my heart
and the sun said
no go

I said to the air
comfort me
and the air said
no go

I said to the earth
bury me
and the earth said
yes, I will

This

for which I am not paid
the hunger out of my mind
the debt I have forsworn
the day I live through
and am paid nothing
and am given nothing
except what I tell myself
again and again to myself
this that I am hampered with
that I am told to forgo and not continue with
yet still I wear the same black coat
and I walk the streets with the same ardor
because a bird in the bush is better
and a chicken in the pot is better
than no bird at all and no chicken ever
despite what they tell me in the house of the prophet
despite what I know about the world and its desiccation
yet I am pledged to this even the earthquake come
even the dislocations even the running in the streets naked
I am pledged to this no matter what the outcome
I am pledged to this no matter what they tell me

ship his body back

ship his body back
he didn't like New York
anyway send him home
where he was killed here and now we get rid of him
because he was anyway too naïve and didn't know how
to talk to people imagine getting into an argument
with a crazed man in a dangerous part of the neighborhood among the trees
of November in a park at 10:45 p.m. how stupid can person be
to come to New York from Ohio and live here for six years and do that
kill him and ship him home

take off
this last letter
to a dead man
because I want to say this
I want to say this
yes I knew him
or why would I write to him
no he will not answer
how could he answer
yes I am sorry about it and sick about it
yes I am completely sad
yes I don't know what will happen now
no there is no way to get away from it
yes a man is dead and he was my friend
yes this will be the last letter I will ever write to him
yes the shock is beyond reason
yes there is never any sense to a murder like that
yes I never thought that such a thing could happen
yes it happened
no there is nothing we can do about it now
yes my friend is dead and this is the last letter I will ever write to him

the ground has him
and that is good
the sky has him
and that is good
the grass has got him
and that is very good
the sea has him the sun has him
and that is good, that is good
and we have lost him, we have lost him
and that is the best

what can you say
speaking to the air
when a man is killed
the air is killed
and when you are alive
the air is alive
what can you say
speaking to the air
that has not been said
that the air has not held

The Last Thing

you are the last thing you will know
the eyes and hands identical
to what they always were, you are
the last sensation you will feel
taste in your mouth breath in your throat
you are the final resting place
of your own final resting place
and everything you are will be
identical to what it was
when what you are is finished; you
are the last thing you will come to

Quandary

body my body, horse and dog
shall I take you with me, wag
my tail and bark, or bleat and bray
body my body, what to say
except that you are what I wear
and almost all that I have here
body my body, what to do
when you're done with me, and I with you

If He Wants Us, He Can Have Us

we're all going belly up
into the great nowhere
heaven or hell is what they say
but I say so long
it's been good to know you, lithesome thing
that we call life, this cage of skin
that was my body, and shall be what
bare bones and dust, goodbye old boy
it's almost time to meet the man
who rules the world, hello hello
funny, you don't look Jewish
I swear I'd know you anywhere
you piece of shit, you god, you geek

Options

there is a pamphlet
that tells you
what your options are
when you have kidney failure
there is hemodialysis
and there is peritoneal dialysis
and there is a transplant
if you can get a transplant
and there is the no-treatment option
which according to the pamphlet
is not so bad
if you choose that option
you just get sort of tired
and then you die

To My Transplanted Kidney

we've been together nine years now
and it's been good
it's almost like you've become a part of me
although I know you're really not mine
that it's just a kind of lifetime loan
and the pills I take fool you into feeling you belong where you are
stay that way, old chap, don't go bad on me
just keep cleaning that blood by filtering those wastes
after all, it's what you were born to do
why should you care where you're doing it
I'm eternally grateful to the wonderful guy you used to work for
who I didn't even know, but he's gone now, and if you've gotten
    attached to me, so what
this arrangement keeps *you* alive too
it's you and me kid, side by inside, stuck on each other till the end

Subway Heaven

I like the smell of the lollipops
that these Spanish women sitting next to me on the subway
are sucking as they talk in their hot sexy fast language
with their black net stockings touching against my leg
what kind of heaven have I stumbled into surrounded by these women
sucking lollipops speaking Spanish sitting next to me in the subway
leaning over letting me look and me smelling that sweet sexy candy
listening to their fast-talking Spanish real hot stuff to go home with the
    thought of them

The Oldest Philosopher in the World

The oldest philosopher in the world sat on a stone. No one listened to him anymore, which was okay with him. He smoked a long pipe and didn't move much, just stuck to his stone, looked up at the stars at night, and let the sun sear his skin all the long days. When I came to see him, he was sort of dangling from his stone, holding on with one hand, the pipe almost falling out of his mouth. I gently adjusted the pipe and pushed him up further on the stone so he wouldn't fall off.

"Thanks," said the oldest philosopher in the world, sitting up higher on the stone and staring into my eyes.

"Don't mention it," I said, "it's the least I could do. I have come here from another country, and from another time, to ask for your help in getting me through the world."

The oldest philosopher in the world turned away, brushed a tear from his cheek, and blew his nose into his handkerchief with a sound like thunder. "Excuse me," he said, "these allergies are killing me."

"I understand" I said, "but I must know if you can help me."

"Help you?" he said. "Young man, I am the oldest philosopher in the world. Now, what is your problem? And be quick about it, this stone is scraping my ass like glass."

"I'm sorry," I said, "but I have come to you to identify my problem. It is, after all, my life that we are talking about."

At this, the old philosopher slid off his stone, spun around in a cartwheel, and hopped back up on his perch as if nothing had happened, the pipe still in his mouth.

"Pretty good, you old fucker," I said, "but of what use is this to me?"

The oldest philosopher looked at me as if I was the dumbest piece of humanity he had ever laid his eyes on in his entire long life. "You imbecile," he said gently, "do you not realize that I have just shown you the secret of all existence, and almost broke my fucking head in the process?"

"Master," I said, kneeling in submission, "but of course I know that. I only answered in keeping with my role as a dumb student who comes to see the oldest philosopher in the world and is unable to understand him. In fact, I understand you very well, you old bastard, your actions and your words are as clear to me as the sun."

"Okay, bozo," said the venerable old man, smiling broadly, "now you're talking. Now go back to where you came from, wherever the fuck that is, and tell my message to the world. But get it right this time, will you, you asshole of assholes."

"Why sure, bubba," I said, turning to go, a look of intense satisfaction on my face. For now I knew what to do and how to do it, and whether or not I got through the rest of my life successfully, I could surely not reproach the oldest philosopher in the world for not having shown me the way.

The Summoning

in my future
I stand ringing a bell
at the border of a huge forest
lost animals gather around me
it is the way I want it to be
one ring of the bell
one silence after

When it Matters

what a silly thing
poetry
who cares about it
the weeds
the weeds care
they grow and grow
we are like the weeds
we care about poetry
it grows in us
it covers us
it undresses us
and we will go naked like that
into our poetic graves
and they will care about us then
and about poetry
finally, they will care about poetry

With the Thousand-Year-Old Woman

it's an experience
to be with her
even for one night

to speak about the past
how much she remembers
how little she has forgotten

she draws me to her
and I can smell the sweetness of the centuries in her hair
it is at times like these that I realize how beautiful she is

I will not let go of her
even if we are together for only one night
time is nothing when it comes to such things

Amazing Queens

when I first came to Queens I thought
well, this is different
there are tigers in the streets there are lions leaping
elephants are climbing the telephone poles
it's an amazing place, I'm really glad I moved here
in Brooklyn there were dogs and cats and that was it
in Queens there are zebras slithering down every alley
it's amazing how moving from Brooklyn to Queens can change your
    perspective

Wallace Stevens in Queens

I have thought of you and thought of you
but none of my thoughts have led to anything real

it is only the roar of the number 7 train
taking me to the World's Fair, that can lead me to what I want

here, so far from home, from the familiar country of the mind
high above the streets of Queens, and the lives that are lived in those streets

I feel the full flush of the cityscape, the rough and tumble of this nether land
and I am finally immersed, not so much in Queens itself, but, rather, in the
    idea of it

How to Become the Poet Laureate of Queens

don't talk
about New York
set your sights
on Jackson Heights
start gushing
over Flushing
be the first
to write about Elmhurst
there's nothing to hide
there's Sunnyside
it's not that hard
to wax poetic over Queens Boulevard
apply some soothing verbal unction
to Broadway Junction
huzza wazza
Queens Plaza
sing gloria gloria
to Astoria
listen to the lark
in Ozone Park
Queens über alles
including Hollis
don't forsake her
write about Jamaica
don't be a poetic loner
write about Corona
have some Aristotelian fear and pity
for Long Island City
extend your reach
to Howard Beach
record the thrills
of Forest Hills
if your poem begins
in St. Albans

let it close
in Fresh Meadows
be a poetry maven
write about Woodhaven
don't write dreck
write about Little Neck
and when you've had your fill
relax in Richmond Hill
and finally, what all this means
is, if you follow these instructions, you can become the poet laureate of Queens

What They Want

isn't poetry
no what they want
is something else smooth language
or something to assuage to help
them live a little longer without having to
notice anything what they want is drivel
for their selfishness celebrations of the ephemeral
moment what they want they always get
always and never because of the pity of it the pain
of it what they want they never really have
they only think they do blind stupid angels
of their own destruction what they want is what they get
in spades and they can have it I don't care
a hoot for what they want I can only give them what I've got

At the Bottom of the Mountain

the poetry editor
fell off a a mountain
he lay bleeding and half-alive on the rocks below
which is where I came upon him as I was writing this poem
this poem that I was going to send to him and here he was
bleeding and dying at my feet fancy meeting you here
Tojo, I said, thought you'd be home editing not climbing mountains
aren't you the guy who's always sending my work back with comments
    about how it doesn't quite make it
and here you are dying right in the middle of my poem
I don't think you're going to make it pal
and I finished the job by stamping his face with my feet
then I noticed that his pockets were full of self-addressed envelopes
holy shit, I said, maybe he accepted one of my poems
I looked through them and sure enough there was one addressed to me
I ripped it open and there were my poems with another note about them
    not quite being there
you too pal, I said, you're not quite there either anymore, and I gave him
    one last kick in the head and walked away whistling

The Last Straw

now even the fucking Pope has published a book of poems
gut yuntiff puntiff o to be a prelate
and published at last how wonderful of him
to enter the lists of poets this is all we need more holy hell
to run into the ground of the New Yorker and Poetry Chicago and all the other literary thugs
with their stinking priesthoods full of their own soggy self-laden papal bull
isn't it enough that the Academy and the Society all bow down to the handlers and Vendlers
so now we have the Pope himself the poet extraordinaire and what is a poor sap like me who can't get shit published supposed to do buy his book or kiss his goddamn ring

Rant

what for poetry
why do we do this shit
what are we trying to accomplish
why are we bothering with it
what is it all about
it's like humping a streetlight
there's nothing to it
there's nothing in it
there's no reason to work at it
what is wrong with me
why am I like this
why am I doing this
it's stupid
it's hopeless
forget it
please, give me a chance
give me a chance to say something
give me a chance to stop writing poetry
I want to stop writing poetry
I want to say something
I want to say something important
I don't want to write a poem
please, no more poetry
I've had it with poetry
enough already with the poetry
say something
let me say something
please, please, let me say something

Reflections on Names in the News

I used to go out with a girl named Amy. She was weird. But I don't want to get into that now. I want to talk about the Amys that have been in the news.

First there was Amy Fisher. You remember her. A sexy young thing in cut-off jeans who was working as a teenage call girl. She shot her pimp boyfriend Joey Buttafuoco's wife in the face, but the wife didn't die. Amy did seven years for that one, and when she got out she became a porn star and now she's a stripper. Good for her—she was kind of rehabilitated. At least she's not shooting people anymore.

Then there was Amy Bishop, who was neither young nor sexy. She was a Harvard-trained neurobiologist who was denied tenure at a university in Alabama. So she stood up at a faculty meeting and shot three professors dead and wounded three others and only stopped shooting because the gun jammed. She called her husband from jail after and asked if the kids had done their homework.

Neither of these two Amys are particularly amiable, except maybe Amy Fisher when she's doing her stripping act. Amy Bishop had better aim so she was more successful at shooting. I prefer Amy Fisher because she's sexy and fun while Amy Bishop is just your typical disgruntled professor who went over the edge. Her husband said he still loves her. I guess it's like the song, "Once in love with Amy, always in love with Amy."

Shortly after the Amy Bishop incident, a man named Joseph Stack crashed a plane into an IRS building because he was angry at the IRS. My last name is Stock, only one letter difference from Stack, and I'm not a fan of the IRS either. And like I said, I once went out with a girl named Amy. So do I have anything to do with these names in the news? And how come two women named Amy are shooting people? Is this all aimless speculation or am I on to something?

Ezra Pound said that poetry is news that stays news. Is this a poem?

Draconian Measures

It was decided to round people up and put them in sealed cabins to prevent the spread of gossip. The amount of rumor-mongering and lies that were about was considered positively dangerous to the entire community. Cabins were built and sealed off from each other by a new kind of plastic tape which, once applied, could not be removed. Sealed in their little cabins, the people were at first quite content. After all, it was they who suffered most from all the lies and rumors. For a while there was a peaceful silence in the village. Then it became known that one man had broken the seal on his cabin, come out into the light, and called his neighbor a buffoon and a glutton. This started a chain reaction of people breaking the supposedly unbreakable seals on the cabins and the rumor mill was alive and running again.

Special mouth clamps were then devised and fitted on the people's mouths. The clamps could be opened to eat but not to talk and automatically slammed shut when enough food had been taken in. People were so amazed by how the clamps worked, they wanted to tell each other about them, but of course were prevented from doing so by the clamps themselves. Again, peace returned to the village, as each person managed to live in silence and not tell tales on his neighbor. Until, one day, one of the villagers figured out how to talk while eating and was able to get a sentence out before the clamps slammed shut after ingestion of sufficient food. This was, needless to say, the beginning of the end. Soon the whole town had learned how to talk while eating, and the rumors began again. In no time, clamps or no clamps, the town was buzzing with the usual slander and poisonous hearsay.

So special types of chains were made, and these chains were attached to the cabins, and the people were attached to the chains. When a person spoke, the chain would snap his head back and cause the words to go flying up in the air, unheard by anybody. The people were at first fascinated by the chain mechanism and felt a euphoric surge at the snapping back of their heads and the flying away of their words. There was a magical quality to the experience, like being on a breathtaking ride in an amusement park. Gradually, however, as they felt the inability to communicate with each other, the people began to dislike the chains. While there was a relative calm in the village due to the lack of slander, the confining nature of this latest measure was more than they could take. Who knows what might have happened, perhaps an open rebellion, had not one ingenious villager discovered a way to retrieve his words before the chain snapped his head back completely, thus making them decipherable. Soon the method was being passed on from one person to the next and the silence that had pervaded the village was again broken. Despite the chains, the villagers were slandering each other as before, while still enjoying the gay snapping of the head, which by then had become a local sport.

Thus, just as the laws of the sealed cabins and the clamped mouths had been repealed, now the edict of the chained heads was nullified. The people were set free, and slander was to be allowed unless it reached a point where further measures were thought to be practicable. The people reacted with a kind of nostalgia. Sealed cabins and mouth clamps became prized objects and drew high prices at collectors' auctions. But most highly valued were the chains, and those who still knew how to work them, to snap their heads back while catching their words before they flew away, became local celebrities. As for the rumors, they actually began to die down as people united in a group memory of the days of the Draconian measures. The topic of conversation that was most popular was how each one had coped in the old days, sealed in cabins or chained to walls or trying to talk while eating before the clamps slammed shut. It seemed that the people now lived in a state of after-shock, remembering how it was and respecting each other for having lived through a perilous time. The delight the people took in talking about how they survived in these situations drew them closer and, at least for a time, drove the gossip from their hearts.

About the Author

Norman Stock's first book, *Buying Breakfast For My Kamikaze Pilot*, was published by Gibbs Smith in 1994 as winner of the Peregrine Smith Poetry Contest. His poems have appeared in *The New Republic, College English, The New York Quarterly, The New England Review, Denver Quarterly, Verse*, and many other magazines, as well as in anthologies and textbooks. The recipient of awards from the Writer's Voice, Poets & Writers' Maureen Egen Writers Exchange, the Bennington Writing Workshops, and the Tanne Foundation, he has also been a Bread Loaf fellow, a Sewanee scholar, and a finalist for Poet Laureate of Queens. Formerly the Acquisitions Librarian at Montclair State University, from which he retired in 2005, he lives with his wife, Lydia Chang, a clinical psychotherapist, in Jackson Heights, New York.

About NYQ Books™

NYQ Books™ was established in 2009 as an imprint of The New York Quarterly Foundation, Inc. Its mission is to augment the New York Quarterly poetry magazine by providing an additional venue for poets already published in the magazine. A lifelong dream of NYQ's founding editor, William Packard, NYQ Books™ has been made possible by both growing foundation support and new technology that was not available during William Packard's lifetime. We are proud to present these books to you and hope that you will continue to support The New York Quarterly Foundation, Inc. and our poets and that you will enjoy these other titles from NYQ Books™:

Barbara Blatner	*The Still Position*
Amanda J. Bradley	*Hints and Allegations*
rd coleman	*beach tracks*
Joanna Crispi	*Soldier in the Grass*
Ira Joe Fisher	*Songs from an Earlier Century*
Sanford Fraser	*Tourist*
Tony Gloeggler	*The Last Lie*
Ted Jonathan	*Bones & Jokes*
Richard Kostelanetz	*Recircuits*
Iris Lee	*Urban Bird Life*
Kevin Pilkington	*In the Eyes of a Dog*
Jim Reese	*ghost on 3rd*
F. D. Reeve	*The Puzzle Master and Other Poems*
Jackie Sheeler	*Earthquake Came to Harlem*
Jayne Lyn Stahl	*Riding with Destiny*
Shelley Stenhouse	*Impunity*
Tim Suermondt	*Just Beautiful*
Douglas Treem	*Everything so Seriously*
Oren Wagner	*Voluptuous Gloom*
Joe Weil	*The Plumber's Apprentice*
Pui Ying Wong	*Yellow Plum Season*
Fred Yannantuono	*A Boilermaker for the Lady*
Grace Zabriskie	*Poems*

Please visit our website for these and other titles:

www.nyqbooks.org

www.ingramcontent.com/pod-product-compliance
Lightning Source LLC
LaVergne TN
LVHW011426080426
835512LV00005B/299